THE
GOOD EGG

HERB PETERSON,
THE EGG MCMUFFIN
—— AND ——
THE SECRET INGREDIENTS
OF INNOVATION

DAVID PETERSON
AND ANN MARSH

Peterson 6

I dedicate this labor of love to my incredible family,
beautiful wife Sue, Whitney, Parker, Lakey and Matt.

–D.P.

CONTENTS

FOREWORD

FRED L. TURNER,
HONORARY CHAIRMAN, McDONALD'S

Over the course of six decades, more than 12,000 entrepreneurs have helped build McDonald's into the organization you see today. They are our unsung heroes. Few people know their stories.

The Good Egg spotlights one of these heroes: Herbert R. Peterson. The breakfast sandwich Herb introduced may be small enough to hold in your hand, but its impact has been significant. Before the Egg McMuffin, McDonald's was in a formative period—limited menu, primarily carryout, no drive-thrus and only a few stores with seating. We were well known for our hamburgers, fries and shakes. And during our first twenty years, we did not serve a hot breakfast. Some of our stores opened at 11 a.m. with some coffee and pastry. A California competitor, Jack in the Box, had a sandwich similar to the Egg McMuffin, however, and Ray Kroc, always a competitor with vision, believed breakfast represented an opportunity for McDonald's.

Herb wanted to serve a breakfast product unique to McDonald's, and so he based his idea on a quick-service, eggs benedict-type of product. He presented his idea to Ray in 1971, along with frozen orange juice with a little bit of pulp. From the first bite, Ray realized the Egg McMuffin could help McDonald's get into breakfast. Herb helped found a great product and was also instrumental in the development of what became the "egg ring." I'm proud to say my wife, Patty, came up with its memorable name.

In 1975, the national rollout of the Egg McMuffin was complete, and the following year we launched a national advertising campaign around the Egg McMuffin, thanks to McDonald's President Ed Schmitt and Chief Marketing Officer Paul Schrage.

Within a few years, breakfast came to account for 15 percent of McDonald's restaurant sales in the United States, and McDonald's became a significant factor in the breakfast market. Today, the Egg McMuffin still has potential to help us grow our breakfast in markets around the world.

Thanks to Herb Peterson—positive and upbeat, a true McMarketing man—the Egg McMuffin makes people smile and makes a healthy, easy and tasty breakfast. The Egg McMuffin is one demonstration of Herb's talent—and so is the McDonald's franchise he built and ran with his talented son, David.

INTRODUCTION

DAVID PETERSON

I count myself extremely blessed because, not long ago, as my father made his transition from earth to heaven, I was present. I was afforded the opportunity to talk with him, laugh with him, pray with him and even lay next to him as I said goodbye. Over the course of those few, surreal days, I had time to reflect on the beautiful life my father lived. My father, Herb Peterson, loved life, and he loved a few particular people and things with wild abandon.

First and most important, he loved my mom. Less than two years after he passed, in fact, she followed him. I'd say my mother died from a broken heart; she just didn't want to be without my father anymore. For sixty-one years they were inseparable. In an age when divorce is the norm, they simply would not leave each other's sides. They ate together, traveled together and laughed together. Working as a team, they raised a beautiful family that started with my three older sisters, Sally and Susan (the twins) and Barbie, and concluded with me. Their family then expanded to thirteen grandchildren and three great-grandchildren. Having survived World War II, Dad didn't take any of us for granted. He loved every moment we shared together.

Second, my dad loved people. Oh, how he loved people. After his passing, the sheer volume of emails, voice mails, notes and blogs that poured in from everyone he touched served as a testament to this fact. From Beijing, China, to Oakbrook, Illinois, everyone had a Herb story to share, and we, in my family, loved hearing them all.

Third, my dad loved McDonald's. Boy, did he love McDonald's. The people who work at McDonald's like to say some people have ketchup in their veins. Well, Dad was one of them. Other than Ray Kroc, the founder of McDonald's and one of my father's best friends, I don't think I've met anyone who loved the Golden Arches more than my father did. As his son and business partner at our six-restaurant franchise in Santa Barbara and Goleta, California, I watched my father imbue everything he did with this passion.

Of course, Dad's love for McDonald's extended to his baby, the Egg McMuffin. Dad loved the fact that his humble creation helped McDonald's enter the breakfast business and secure a dominance it still retains to this day. He loved his creation's unforgettable name. He loved how it tasted. Finally, he loved sharing it with others and, over nearly forty years, reveled in giving thousands and thousands away for free. He loved the fact that Egg McMuffins made people happy.

No matter what adventure God has called you to, I hope you find this short tale of my father's creation—and life—useful and inspiring. I hope you can take hold of some of these simple lessons and live a little as my father did: full of smiles, full of love and full of good cheer.

Enjoy!

David Peterson

P.S. Even though this is a very personal and emotional story for me, it's also more than that. My dad belonged to our entire community and not just his family members. Because this is a story for everyone, my coauthor and I chose not to tell it in my voice, but in the third person.

PROLOGUE

ONE SUNNY AFTERNOON . . .

One sunny afternoon in 1971, shortly before Christmas, Ray Kroc walked into the McDonald's restaurant on Upper State Street in Santa Barbara, California.

As the company founder, Ray occasionally liked to drop in unannounced at one of his 1,900 McDonald's restaurants around the country. If he found the conditions wanting, he wasn't above picking up discarded cigarette butts or grabbing a hose and washing down a parking lot to show the franchisee what he expected.

But this was a different sort of visit. Ray was not only expected, he'd also been invited—by the store's owner, Herb Peterson, who wanted to show him a new idea for the company. Ray knew that Herb was always full of ideas, but he was skeptical. His franchisees were constantly throwing out ideas for new menu items, but only rarely did the ideas ever amount to anything. Even Ray understood how difficult it could be to convert any of them into a success. All of Ray's own ideas for desserts over the years—every single one of them—had bombed.

As Ray made his way through the restaurant, which was busy with lunchtime customers, he blinked at the unusual sight of Herb standing next to a man wearing a tall, white chef's hat. With them was Bob Kelly, Herb's son-in-law and director of operations. The three men looked expectantly at Ray.

"Hello, Ray," Herb said in his deep, raspy voice, hoping he didn't appear anywhere near as nervous as he felt.

"Herb, if this is an idea for a new uniform, the answer is no," Ray said with a laugh, nodding toward the man in the toque.

Herb shook his head. "I've got something I think you are going to like."

As Ray joined Herb behind the counter, the "chef" served him up a plate with two freshly toasted sides of English muffin on it. One was topped with an egg cooked in a perfect circle, a slice of melted cheese and a round slice of Canadian bacon. A pat of butter was busy melting down into the surface of the other side of the muffin.

Herb explained that his creation could be eaten with a fork and knife or the two halves could be joined to make a sandwich. Ray chose the latter and took a bite.

As it happened, Ray wasn't particularly hungry that day. He'd already enjoyed lunch in town with some friends. But unbeknownst to Herb, Ray had good reason to be paying close attention. Back at the company headquarters outside Chicago, Ray and his colleagues had been discussing the very problem that Herb's creation was meant to solve.

Herb watched Ray bite down into the small sandwich he had so painstakingly developed.

As he chewed, Ray looked at the faces of the three men. Though vital as ever, he was older than all of them—nearly sixty-nine. Even before he opened his first restaurant at age fifty-two, he wasn't shy about telling people that he had diabetes and incipient arthritis. He mentioned them almost as badges of honor. In earlier health battles, he'd lost part of his thyroid gland and all of his gall bladder. But none of that managed to slow him down. He still had an appetite for innovation equal to his appetite for delicious food. "I'm still green and growing," he liked to say.

Ray's hearing wasn't in any better shape than his joints. When he was excited, he sometimes spoke so loudly, his words came out in a shout. Herb and Bob watched anxiously, unable to discern Ray's opinion.

At last, Ray swallowed and then, suddenly, smacked the countertop with his hand.

"I like it!" he exclaimed, loudly enough to turn several customers' heads. "We could open the doors earlier. Let's do it!"

Herb and Bob broke into broad grins. Ray proceeded to finish the sandwich. Then despite the full lunch in his stomach, he asked for another and finished that one, too.

Herb's spirits soared. He knew Ray's approval might mean the beginning of new chapter for him, his company and his customers. *Might.* A long road still lay ahead.

He flashed back to all the false starts, experimentation and serendipity that had brought him this far.

Even if it didn't work out in the end, it had already been a bit of a fairy tale.

1

LISTEN FOR THE KNOCK
ON THE DOOR

O nce upon a time and long ago, there was a breakfast crisis across the land. Basically, people had stopped eating it. It was the early 1970s, and life was starting to move more quickly than ever before. Making a nutritious breakfast didn't rank high on anyone's list. More and more women, including mothers, were taking jobs, which left them little time to toast toast and fry eggs—and most men in those days didn't know a skillet from a hole in the ground. The people considered themselves lucky if they were able to grab a banana or a doughnut before they left the house in the morning.

So all over the land, people had terrible hunger pains by the middle of the morning. They were grouchy. They couldn't get their work done properly. Unhappiness was up and productivity was down. Something had to be done.

As it happened, a man named Herb Peterson was watching this problem closely. In a pretty seaside town, this father of four ran three McDonald's restaurants that were very popular—just not at breakfast. His restaurants were famous for their hamburgers, which Herb didn't start serving until 11 a.m. But long before that, as early as 8 a.m., customers were already outside knocking on his windows.

"Hello!" they called to him through the glass. "Can I get a burger?"

Herb would poke his head outside the door and say, "I'm sorry. We open at eleven. Can you please come back then?"

The people at the door were frustrated. Herb was frustrated, too. Here he sat with three big restaurants full of grills, cooking utensils, refrigerators and colorful décors, yet he couldn't help the visitors. He would have loved to make these people breakfast, but that wasn't his job. His job was to make hamburgers and to start serving them for lunch.

Or was it?

What if he could serve breakfast?

He shook his head at the thought. McDonald's was in the lunch-and-dinner business and did quite well at it. He would be afraid even to bring up the subject. Someone else who worked at some other company would have to do it.

But Herb couldn't let go of his idea. He felt he understood something very important. He knew that he wasn't just in the business of serving hamburgers. He was in the business of making people happy. Yet here he was, disappointing them.

What if he *did* come up with the right breakfast idea? It might work. His company might like it. For it to happen, however, he would need to convince many other people that serving breakfast was a good idea. That would be a lot of extra work.

But he was getting ahead of himself.

THE YOLK OF THE MATTER

Heed the hunger.

2

DREAM IT, HATCH IT

The world is full of already-successful products that most people take for granted. People assume either that these products just always existed or that everyone immediately saw their value. But Herb knew that every success is built on a mountain of doubt, persistence and luck.

Take French fries, for example. When the fishing nets came up empty one day in Belgium in the 1600s, the Belgians claim one of their countrymen was the first person to fry up strips of potatoes as a substitute for the main course. Legend has it that British and American soldiers first dubbed them French fries during World War I. Or take the hamburger. A man named Louis Lassen, who had a lunch truck in New Haven, Connecticut, threw together the first one back in 1900. He stuck a beef patty between two pieces of white bread for a harried businessman one day, and the world hasn't been the same since.

Just thinking about how to serve breakfast made Herb anxious—it wouldn't be easy—but also excited. It wouldn't be the first time he'd taken a big risk. He knew it would take courage. He had left a successful career in another field and invested his life savings to open his restaurants. He had sold the house that he and his wife had built outside of Chicago in order to move to California while three of his four children were still living at home.

Herb was a man who believed in possibilities. He put great stock in dreams that some considered far-fetched. His three restaurants were gleaming dreams come true.

But just like his customers, Herb hated to see those restaurants sitting idle every morning. He was paying dearly for his mortgage and other overhead costs, but not getting the maximum return out of them. He needed that income to help repay the investment he made to open his restaurants. McDonald's was still growing fast. Since so many people already loved to eat at these restaurants, he just knew they could come to eat breakfast, too. But he also knew that there was usually a long road between identifying a need and filling it, and he knew it was a road littered with dead projects.

First, Herb would have to figure out what to make. He would need to create a single breakfast that appealed to millions. He needed to find a way to make something out of nothing.

Fortunately, making something out of nothing was how Herb lived his life. He had grown up poor in Chicago during the Depression. His father, a U.S. Marine pilot, had died of yellow fever while training to fight in World War I, when Herb was just three months old. His mother, aunt and grandmother raised him as an only child.

After going to college and serving with the U.S. Marines in World War II, Herb went into advertising. His mind crackled with ideas. He couldn't stop the flow of them. He told friends and coworkers about all the ideas that popped into his head. He doodled a lot of them on napkins and in notebooks.

One of his first clients was the very young McDonald's, which was rapidly becoming famous for its hamburgers, shakes and fries. Herb worked closely alongside the company's founder and top managers. Their goal was to make the company grow and grow and grow. Herb's job was to help them shape the company's first advertising campaigns. He thought up an early advertising slogan, "Quality made fresh every day." He also helped design the first costume for a funny character named Ronald, who became the much-beloved face of the company. It was a dream job for an idea man like Herb.

Herb came to love McDonald's so much that he thought about running one or two of its restaurants. This would mean leaving his successful career as an advertiser, of course, and going from a large national perch to a smaller local one. A lot of people thought Herb was nuts. He was nearly fifty years old and had never worked in a restaurant before.

In a couple of years, Herb proved them wrong. No doubt others would think he was nuts to think he could restore breakfast to a land where the people no longer knew how to make it themselves.

THE YOLK OF THE MATTER

Dreams are great—if you're sleeping.
But to make them come true, you have to be awake.

3

LOVE WHAT YOU MAKE AND MAKE WHAT YOU LOVE

One thing Herb understood instinctively was that his customers would want a breakfast food that was as convenient as the hamburgers they enjoyed for lunch and dinner—something they could eat by hand. But what?

Fate intervened. Early one morning, Herb came whistling through the back door of one of his restaurants. The employees were preparing everything for lunch. Herb smelled eggs sizzling on the griddle. His son-in-law, Bob Kelly, who worked for him at the time, and a couple of other guys were making themselves a bite to eat by frying up eggs and sticking them inside hamburger buns.

They offered one to Herb.

He looked at the makeshift breakfast sandwich in his hand. It was a portable breakfast, even if it was a sloppy one. Herb took a bite. It was all right—just an egg sandwich.

Herb wondered if he couldn't make a breakfast sandwich that was a little tastier and tidier. One of his competitors, a company called Jack in the Box that operated restaurants in just a few states, was already selling something similar: a breakfast sandwich on a hamburger bun. Herb wasn't surprised it hadn't caught on.

He felt confident he could make something better—something people would start thinking about first thing in the morning, something that could generate a little healthy obsession like Herb's own craving for a plate of eggs benedict when he woke up.

Herb had long had a secret love affair with eggs benedict. The dish wasn't just delicious, it was elegant. And Herb had a great love of elegance. Maybe it was the result of not eating out or not having many new clothes as a kid. Or maybe it was because he spent so many years living in muddy foxholes during World War II. Whatever the reason, Herb loved to go out. He ate at his own establishments daily, of course, but he also frequented the fancier restaurants in town. And he dressed elegantly, too. Every day of his life, he left his house looking like a distinguished English gentleman, in suits or sharp sport coats paired with pressed slacks. He wore brightly colored ties and, frequently, pink shirts. When it came to the first meal of the day, he usually ordered eggs benedict. It was a breakfast as elegant as his attire.

Even though his restaurants served lots of hard-working, middle-class folks who probably had never heard of eggs benedict, Herb was always coming up with ways to offer them the sort of service they might find in a five-star hotel. He was staunchly opposed to anything that seemed "schlocky"—one of his favorite words. He designed many of the interiors of his restaurants himself, paying special attention to color. He put out rows of fresh, yellow mums. When he called each of his restaurants at 6 p.m. every evening, he wanted to know just two things: "What are sales?" and "Has anyone watered the mums?" He opened doors for customers, especially mothers with children. He would bring coffee to customers' tables and sit and talk with them.

He spent much of his time holding court in those restaurants. When he was younger, he had dreamed of becoming a professional singer and performer. Now that he fed people food for a living, those restaurants became his stage.

When Herb first thought about serving breakfast at this special place, he wanted only the best; he wanted to serve something to rival his hamburgers' popularity—something everyone else could love as much as he did. Herb kept picturing his son-in-law Bob's egg sandwich and the egg sandwich his competitor sold. Both were built like a burger on a bun. Buns were the obvious choice. But buns were for hamburgers. He didn't want his breakfast to look—or taste—like a hamburger. So what else could he use?

Toast? But pieces of bread were too large, and they crumbled everywhere. Bagels? Too heavy. Then Herb thought of his favorite meal. What if he served breakfast on an English muffin? Herb decided to give it a try. Unfortunately, he couldn't find any English muffins. In those days, many grocery stores, especially in California, didn't carry them. And who could blame them? English muffins had been invented some two hundred years ago, and more or less accidentally, half a world away in, of course, England. Servants used to make them for themselves out of leftover scraps of dough. Hot out of the oven, the "muffins" were supposed to be roughly pulled apart instead of sliced. These scrappy muffins were so tasty that they didn't stay downstairs in the servants' quarters for long. Once the folks upstairs discovered them, they insisted on having the muffins served in the dining room. People of all classes became enamored of the muffins, and, in time, they were so popular that "muffin men" roamed the streets of England selling them from trays supported by straps around the necks.

The first English muffins made their way to America in the late nineteenth century, first to New York and later to Chicago, which became home of the popular Bays English Muffin. Chicago, of course, was also the home of Herb, who had grown up eating English muffins. When he couldn't find the English muffins in California, he called the Bays people in Chicago, and they shipped him a box.

Without realizing it—and, in fact, while associating English muffins with haute cuisine—Herb had picked a baked good with origins as humble as his own. And wouldn't it be great if Herb found a new way to reintroduce it to the hungry masses?

Then he turned his attention to the meat. That was easier. Once Herb settled on eggs benedict for his inspiration, he knew he would use Canadian bacon, even though most people were no more familiar with Canadian bacon at the time than they were with English muffins. He could already hear the response of some people at his company. "You want to do what? Make a breakfast sandwich with bread from Europe and meat from Canada?" But Herb was beginning to feel he was on to something.

He placed a call to Chicago again, this time to one of his and his wife's many friends, Oscar Mayer. (Yes, there actually *is* a man named Oscar Mayer). Most people knew him for his bologna, but Mayer's company sold all kinds of meat products. Mayer was only too glad to oblige Herb and sent his friend a thirty-pound log of the best Canadian bacon. When it arrived, Herb lugged it into the back of his Upper State Street store and rolled up his sleeves.

THE YOLK OF THE MATTER

To find your way,
sometimes you have to go out of your way.

4

BREAK LOTS OF EGGS

When Herb started experimenting, he couldn't imagine how to transform eggs benedict into a sandwich that could be eaten by hand. In fact, his favorite breakfast posed several challenges.

As with syrupy pancakes and waffles, the classic eggs benedict is eaten with a knife and fork. It consists of a toasted, open-faced English muffin, both sides of which are topped with a slice of Canadian bacon and a poached egg. Then bright yellow hollandaise sauce is poured generously over everything.

Like many people, Herb liked the eggs on his eggs benedict undercooked. That way he could pierce the center with his fork and release the yolk to flow out and mingle with the yellow of the hollandaise sauce. It made a colorful mess, which was always part of the fun of eggs benedict. So was cleaning it up using a doll-sized mop made by attaching a bit of English muffin to your fork. At first, Herb was determined to figure out a way to reproduce this experience for his customers.

Herb's wife, Barbara, laughed at the idea of her husband experimenting with his new dish. She knew better than anyone that Herb could not cook to save his life. Once, when she was away, Herb called to ask, "Barb, do I have wait until the water bubbles to put in the hot dogs?"

But by now, Herb was too driven to solve the problem with breakfast to let a detail like his complete ignorance of culinary technique get in the way. Away from his home kitchen, where Barbara's gourmet cooking held sway, he took over the kitchen at his Upper State Street restaurant early in the morning.

Herb felt emboldened for two other reasons. One was Jim Delligatti, who ran restaurants for Herb's company out in Pittsburgh. Like Herb, Jim was creative and eager to expand his business. Five years earlier, in 1967, he succeeded in convincing his company to begin selling a new double-decker hamburger called the Big Mac, which became a tremendous success. Then there was Lou Groen, another operator out in Cincinnati, who came up with a fish sandwich, which came to be called the Filet-O-Fish, for his Catholic customers to eat on Fridays when they traditionally gave up meat. If Lou and Jim could do it, maybe Herb could, too.

At first, Herb tried to make eggs the eggs benedict way, by poaching them. This soon proved too difficult, and he concluded that since his restaurants were already equipped with grills, it would be much easier to fry the eggs. But every time he fried an egg, the whites spread out into an unpredictable splotch, too big for the English muffin he had nominated to contain it. After failing several times to corral the egg's perimeter with his spatula, Herb stared hopelessly at the grill.

Wouldn't it be nice if he could fry eggs every time in a perfect circle just the size of an English muffin?

Herb's mind leapt to the trails around town, where his neighbors rode horses. He figured there had to be a blacksmith somewhere nearby. There was. Herb paid the man a visit with an English muffin in hand. Before he knew it, the blacksmith fashioned a perfect black iron ring with sides about an inch tall. The ring was welded to a long metal handle.

Herb took the contraption back to his restaurant, sat the ring on the grill and cracked an egg into it. The egg fried up into a perfectly round circle only slightly smaller than the diameter of the muffin.

With a little ingenuity—and a lot of broken shells—Herb had tamed the egg. He placed a slice of Canadian bacon, along with this perfectly circular fried egg, inside a toasted English muffin and spooned a little hollandaise over it. He expected many people would eat this breakfast open-faced with a knife and fork, the way he liked it, but he wanted them to have the option of eating it like a sandwich. When Herb picked it up, he noticed that it fit very nicely in the palm of his hand.

But when he took a bite, a river of hollandaise sauce and the contents of the yolk ran, thick and gooey, down his sleeve.

THE YOLK OF THE MATTER

Sometimes it takes new shapes to contain new ideas.

5

IF THE SAUCE DOESN'T FIT, DON'T WEAR IT!

Herb thought about all the little decisions that had gotten him this far and realized he'd have to make a few more. A mess on a plate of eggs benedict is one thing; a mess down your arm is another.

The yolk was easy to fix. Despite egg benedict tradition and his own personal preference, Herb decided the eggs in this sandwich would have to be cooked firm. There was just no way around it.

The hollandaise sauce was another matter. In fact, the hollandaise didn't just have one strike against it, it had several. Not only did it run, but it also was made with barely cooked yolks. These required a delicate preparation, with skillful whipping at precisely the right temperature. Even if his company *was* able to mass produce hollandaise, he would still be serving undercooked eggs to the public. How could he or his company maintain food-safety standards? Still, Herb couldn't imagine making eggs benedict without hollandaise sauce.

Fortunately, most people didn't share his opinion. As Herb made up his first egg sandwiches, complete with hollandaise sauce, he offered samples to some of his young coworkers. Many were teenagers who addressed him as Mr. Peterson to be polite but, among themselves, preferred calling him Pops. Their response to hollandaise sauce could be summed up in one word: yuck.

Most had never eaten eggs benedict and weren't familiar with the taste. Made with butter, chili pepper, lemon, and egg yolks, hollandaise sauce has its own unique flavor. Even Herb had to admit it was an acquired one. It turned out that while the

English muffin could travel easily from upper class England to middle class America, hollandaise sauce was going to be stopped at the border.

After coming so far, and after so much trial and error, Herb had to face facts. But his concoction needed something, because without hollandaise sauce, it was just not right.

∞ ∞ ∞

Sometimes all it takes is one thing to pull everything together: the perfect word, the exact tool—or a special ingredient. Herb found the answer to his sauce problem right under his nose. Herb's restaurants were already filled with American cheese for their famous hamburgers. So Herb slapped a piece of Kraft American cheese on top of the egg of his new breakfast sandwich.

He and all his experimental tasters agreed that the result was delicious. The cheese was a perfect fit. And it was fitting that, although England had provided the right bread and Canada the right bacon, America would provide the right substitute for the sauce.

With a thin spread of butter on the English muffin, Herb felt he'd created a dish uniquely suited to solve the problem with breakfast. It fit in the hand. You could eat it on the go. It didn't drip on your hand or clothing. It was so simple, now that he'd finally created it. It was one of those things where you say, "Gee, why didn't I think of this before?" But one of the many interesting aspects of innovation is how hard you sometimes have to work to find the simple solution. Only Herb knew how much inspiration, experimentation and concentration it took to put all the parts together in precisely the right way.

But as complex as the creation process had been to this point, the hard part still lay ahead of him.

THE YOLK OF THE MATTER

One man's sauce is another man's cheese.

6

FIND YOUR FATHER

One important ingredient was still missing. Every creation, no matter how brilliant, needs the support of people who can help it grow. Herb's solution to the breakfast problem was no exception, and neither was Herb the man.

Herb lost his father just after he was out of the egg himself, and he grew up an only child, the center of attention for his mother, his grandmother and his maiden aunt. The four of them lived together in a three-story walk-up apartment with a living room that doubled as Herb's bedroom at night. Herb lived there, on Chicago's North Side, until he graduated from college and left for the war at age twenty-two. Herb didn't lack for strong maternal guidance, but part of him still yearned to fill the gap left inside of him when his father died. Even people with wonderful mothers and fathers often must find another "parent" or two to mentor them and help them grow.

Herb was older than a lot of people—forty-one—when he met his mentor, the man who would affect his life more than Herb ever could have imagined. The man who, it later turned out, would also help him spread his solution to the breakfast problem across the country and, ultimately, the world.

Herb's mentor, Ray Kroc, had just one child, his daughter Marilyn. But, if you count all his restaurants, he sure helped raise a lot of entrepreneurs in his time. Ray was nearly sixty-three when he met Herb, who working in the Chicago advertising firm hired by Ray's company, which was rather small at the time—with 738 locations compared to today's 13,000 domestically and 30,000 globally. Even though people in the youth-oriented advertising industry thought Herb was old, Ray didn't see Herb that way, because he didn't think about age in the usual way. Many years before, he had started his restaurant company at the ripe age of fifty-two. He saw the sort of potential in Herb that he saw in his "younger" self.

Herb first met Ray when he was hired to help find new and creative ways to market and advertise Ray's restaurants to people around the country. Ray liked to say that he didn't trust ad men. But he was drawn to Herb. In his youth, Ray had trained as an ambulance driver to serve in World War I, but the war ended before he could be shipped abroad. So he was impressed that Herb served for four long years in World War II as a U.S. Marine. He also liked the way Herb dressed with real panache. It reminded Ray of his own unique swagger. Back in his youth during the Roaring Twenties, Ray had earned a living playing piano in nightclubs and liked to tell colorful stories of that bygone era.

Herb's wardrobe had similar roots. He'd made his first big mark on the world singing at a famous musical revue, called Waa-Mu, at Northwestern University. Known as "the greatest college show in America," Waa-Mu would later help launch the careers of celebrities like Cloris Leachman, Ann-Margret, and Warren Beatty. Herb made such a splash singing onstage that he thought he might go on to become a performer himself. Though his life took another path, Herb never stopped singing. At a holiday party not long after he and Ray met, Herb listened as Ray played the first few bars of a popular song. Without missing a beat, Herb began singing, "Fly me to the moon, let me play among the stars." With a surprised smile, Ray joined him: "Let me see what spring is like on Jupiter and Mars." It was a fitting sentiment for two friends who loved to perform—and to dream—together.

It was easy to tell when Herb and Ray were together at a party. The feeling was electric, magical. They lit up a room. "Simpatico" was the word one friend used to describe their relationship. They always enjoyed each other's company. Herb shared some of his constantly flowing ideas with Ray to help him grow his company.

Herb admired the man and his restaurants so much that, on the cusp of his own fiftieth birthday, he took a risk and asked Ray if he could come and work for him. Herb wanted to try his hand at running a restaurant or two near his family home in Chicago. In response, Ray smiled and posed Herb a question to which he already knew the answer, "Your wife's name is Barbara, right? Well, we need someone to open restaurants in Santa Barbara, California."

As it happened, Ray owned a ranch not far from Santa Barbara. Although he still lived in Chicago, near the headquarters of his company, he was spending more and more time out West. He liked spending time with Herb and his family. His birthday fell a day before the birth of Herb's son, David, and, for years, the two families often celebrated together.

So Herb and his extended family moved to Santa Barbara to open Herb's first restaurant on October 2, 1968. Once they were out there, they were able to spend even more time with Ray socializing, playing music together, singing, and talking about lunch, dinner and—one day—breakfast.

THE YOLK OF THE MATTER

The road to success is paved with mentors.
Find yours.

7

CHOOSE YOUR SHOT

Part of the reason Herb and Ray got along well is because Herb understood that Ray was a very busy man. Ray was legendary for taking a single successful hamburger restaurant and then, over the years, opening more just like it. McDonald's wasn't all that big when Herb opened his first location in 1969. By then, there were only a little more than 1,200 restaurants. Eventually Ray's company would go on to open more than 30,000 in 118 countries all over the world. So even though they were friends and Herb ran three McDonald's restaurants and lived close to Ray's ranch home, Herb didn't bother him with little details about business. That way, on social occasions, they were free to talk about whatever was on Ray's mind.

But once Herb created the solution to the breakfast problem, he knew the next step was to share it with Ray. He needed to convince his friend and mentor that this small sandwich would be a very good thing for everyone in the company—even if it meant the company would have to make some very big changes to begin selling breakfast.

Herb thought hard about how to present the idea to Ray. He understood the importance of timing, even with good friends. If he fumbled this one, if he got Ray at a bad moment, or if any number of things that he couldn't predict went wrong, he might blow his chance to solve the breakfast problem.

Herb knew he had an advantage. Because Ray liked to spend time in California, he was often in a good mood during his time at his ranch. Sometimes, he would drop in on one of Herb's restaurants unexpectedly just to see how everything was going. On more than one occasion, Herb had pulled into the parking lot to find Ray out hosing down the pavement. On the one hand, it delighted Herb to bump into his friend and mentor. On the other, Herb went on high alert because Ray was his boss, after all, and a stickler for details. Ray never hesitated to point out flaws to Herb or to challenge him with questions.

Herb decided that next time Ray was out in Santa Barbara, he would take the initiative and invite him to pay a special visit.

Herb wasn't aware just how keenly Ray understood the problem with breakfast on the December day that Ray strode into Herb's restaurant on Upper State Street. Ray and his team had permitted a few operators here and there around the country to experiment with stopgap solutions. Some McDonald's restaurants were offering customers orange juice, coffee and sweet rolls in the morning. Ray knew it wasn't enough. He was just waiting to find the perfect means of serving a real breakfast to all the hungry customers who wanted it, but he was treading carefully. He knew just how difficult it could be to introduce a new meal.

The timing of Herb's presentation to Ray couldn't have been better. But although Ray exclaimed "I like it!" somewhat louder than necessary, Herb still knew the success of his egg sandwich was far from guaranteed. Now Ray and Herb would need to find just as effective a way to introduce it to everyone else at McDonald's and, hopefully, everyone else in the world.

THE YOLK OF THE MATTER

Timing isn't everything, but without it,
your hard work may amount to nothing.

8

SERVE BACON,
BE A HAM

Herb started serving his new breakfast sandwich to customers right away during that holiday season. The idea hadn't been officially approved yet, but with Ray's blessing, Herb felt emboldened to push ahead.

At first sales were slow. In a full day, Herb might sell only thirty to forty sandwiches for just fifty-five cents each. But those numbers grew rapidly. The problem with breakfast was solved for a small group of people lucky enough to live near Herb and his three restaurants.

Herb was incredibly excited. He served the first sandwiches like his beloved eggs benedict, open-faced, so that customers could sit down and eat them with a knife and fork if they wanted to. They came in a red cardboard box, covered with clear cellophane instead of a lid.

One morning, Herb picked up the phone at his restaurant on Fairview Street. "What in the $#@!! do you think you are *doing* out there?" a man on the other end of the line wanted to know. He was calling from the company's headquarters in Oak Brook, Illinois. "What is all this about *breakfast*?"

"Well, I should tell you," Herb told the caller. "Ray gave us his blessing."

Herb heard the other line go quiet.

After hanging up, Herb looked at Bob Kelly. Herb smiled with a grin that lit up his round face. Ever since he lost most of his hair, Herb could sometimes resemble one of his favorite foods, the egg. He loved to do impressions of characters that also had balding pates, like W. C. Fields and Colonel Klink, the overwrought German commandant from the TV show *Hogan's Heroes*.

"So," Herb said, doing his best Klink. "Ve veel show zem!"

THE YOLK OF THE MATTER

*When you've got your ducks in a row,
make sure one of them is a really big duck.*

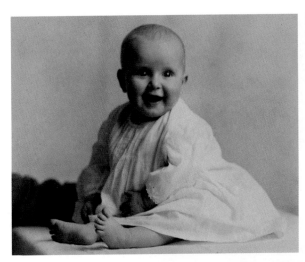

Even when he was only two months old, Herb's joy of life was evident.

Herb in a rare moment of repose between battles in the Pacific Theater during World War II.

Herb and Barbara in the early days—always stylish and often enjoying a good meal together.

One of Herb's first advertising campaigns featured his daughter Barbie and her sisters Susan and Sally.

Proud parents of twins Sally and Susan.

D'ARCY ADVERTISING COMPANY

PRUDENTIAL PLAZA
CHICAGO 1 ILLINOIS

November 20, 1967

Mr. Ray Kroc
Chairman of the Board
MC DONALD'S CORPORATION
Crocker-Citizens Bank Building
6922 Hollywood Boulevard
Hollywood, California

Dear Ray:

I had hoped to have a private moment with you when you were in Chicago last week, but perhaps it's just as well that I put my thoughts down in writing.

For two and a half years I have grown increasingly interested in owning one or more McDonald's units. I have now come to the realization that this is the time to do something about it. I am ready to resign from my present position and give <u>full time</u> to developing what I hope will be one of the successful operations of the future.

The fulfillment of this desire is, of course, contingent upon many things, and the number one important issue is the procurement of a unit or possibly two.

Financially, I can swing the cash requirement for a single unit if the Peterson family practices a little frugality. On the other hand, a very close associate of mine is interested in our forming a partnership, and with his financial capacity we could definitely negotiate two units.

ST. LOUIS • NEW YORK • CHICAGO • CLEVELAND SOUTH B N

Mr. Ray Kroc   -2-   November 20, 1967

From the very personal standpoint of family and friends I'd like to stay in or around Chicago, but the geographical opportunity must come first! If Lake Forest could be opened up from a zoning standpoint, it could be a real bonanza. Lake Forest has nothing like a McDonald's and it is the second largest community by virtue of square miles in the State of Illinois. There's money, homes, churches, schools - everything a good location should have.

If I should be considered for a franchise I would like to discuss the possibility of one of the new building designs and, of course, it would be great to start off with the roast beef sandwich facility!

I hope by now that you can sense my loyalty and interest in McDonald's as well as that of Barbara, who's with me 100% on this. For your information, I am 48 years of age and, in addition to a successful advertising career, I served four years in the Marine Corps during World War II rising to the rank of Major. I'm confident that I can successfully blend the proven assets of service, quality and cleanliness with creative imagination to establish a business that McDonald's and any community will be proud of.

Please bear in mind that I personally will run this operation if I am granted a franchise and I'm open to consideration of any location. I hope to be out in California soon and would welcome the opportunity to talk further with you. In the meantime, if you have any suggestions for action on my part, I'd appreciate hearing from you.

Naturally, I would like to keep all this <u>strictly confidential</u> until such a time as I may be granted a franchise, and then I'll shout it from the housetops. Rest assured that if it doesn't work out I will continue to happily serve McDonald's and D'Arcy.

Sincerely,

Herbert R. Peterson

HRP:ct

Herb's letter to Ray Kroc in 1967, asking to become a McDonald's owner-operator-franchisee.

Herb's favorite diploma:
Class of '73 from
Hamburger University.

McDonald's
HAMBURGER UNIVERSITY
Elk Grove, Illinois

Diploma

Presented to

HERBERT R. PETERSON

who has satisfactorily completed the

ADVANCED OPERATIONS COURSE
and is hereby granted the degree of
"BACHELOR OF HAMBURGEROLOGY"

DATE AUGUST 1968

CLASS 73

A proud Herb on opening day at
the Fairview McDonald's in 1969.

David Peterson with
Little Mac at the Santa
Barbara Zoo.

Herb helped create the Ronald McDonald character in the late 1960s.

The Egg McMuffin, Herb's baby.

Laughter and fun have always been an important part of McDonald's
Santa Barbara and Goleta.

This portrait appeared
in *Life* magazine in 1990.

Even in his eighties, Herb expressed his creative and artistic side.

Family was the most important thing in Herb's life.

A Chinese delegation came to Santa Barbara and spent time with Herb, Barbara, David and David's daughter, Whitney, in 1990. Herb and David helped the members of the delegation get excited about introducing McDonald's to their country.

This photo, Herb's favorite, sat right on his desk where he could see it every day. He couldn't have been more proud of his growing family.

Herb and Barbara's love of life was infectious.

One of David's favorite photos of his father, taken in front of the Milpas Street restaurant.

Traveling in Israel
in the mid-1990s.

As Herb and Barbara grew older, their love for each other did not.

Herb never shied away from telling the Egg McMuffin story.

Monte, David and Herb all dressed up in a few of their many costumes.
Herb always wanted blonde hair.

This picture of Herb and David was used in a McDonald's advertisement in the local paper.

COURTESY ADIAN BRADLEY

The Egg McMuffin license plate that was proudly displayed on all of Herb's cars for the past thirty years.

9

BE NOURISHED
BY NAYSAYERS

As word of Herb's creation spread, what followed was not only excitement, but also fear and confusion. Even some of the best ideas scare people in the beginning. Everyone wondered what the solution to breakfast might mean for their restaurants and their lives.

The McDonald's manager for the western region made a special trip up to Santa Barbara from his base in Los Angeles to visit Herb and try to convince him to stop serving his breakfast sandwich. Herb took the opportunity to try and convince the regional manager of the sandwich's merits. Neither one succeeded in his quest.

Out in Brainard, Minnesota, an eighteen-year-old assistant restaurant manager named Glen Cook took a look at Herb's creation and just couldn't figure it out. Glen had never seen round-cut bacon, an egg cooked in a perfect circle or an English muffin before.

"If I don't know what this is, the customers sure won't either," Glen thought to himself. When he heard people calling it the "poor man's eggs benedict," that didn't clarify things for Glen since he'd never heard of eggs benedict before.

Not far away, in Minneapolis, a sixteen-year-old named Jeff Schwartz, who worked behind the grill, had pretty much the same reaction. "If they serve this in England, then, why are we eating it here?" he wondered. "Why do they think this thing will go?"

Jeff had another, more visceral reaction, too: "I thought, 'Wow, I'm going to have to get up really early—and I'm not a morning person.'"

It took a while for Glen and Jeff and lots of people like them to get used to the solution to the breakfast problem, but they finally did. More than three decades later, in fact, Jeff would become the chief executive officer of McDonald's China and take the lead role in introducing Herb's egg sandwich to a nation of 1 billion people.

As word of the breakfast sandwich spread, the feeling was much the same in many of the approximately 2,700 restaurants in the company. It might be summed up in a single word: "What?!"

At a large regional marketing meeting involving McDonald's franchisees south in Los Angeles, a man who ran about forty restaurants confronted Herb and Bob Kelly.

"You guys are crazy," he told them. "We already have a winning formula, so what's the point of messing with it? Our competitors don't sell breakfast. Why should we?" He could barely keep up with the pace of demand for hamburgers alone. Adding breakfast to the mix was sure to present a logistical nightmare. He and many other franchisees were concerned that breakfast traffic would simply drain visits away from lunch and dinner. He was convinced this breakfast sandwich in particular and breakfast in general, were the dumbest ideas to come down the pike, and he told Herb and Bob as much.

"Do you really think we're going to turn our lights on at 7 a.m.?" he asked them.

Herb wished everyone else could see the tremendous opportunity being presented to them. He wished they could understand that the effort of getting up a few hours earlier everyday would prove more than worth it.

Herb's gut told him that with everyone in his company behind it, this sandwich could indeed fly. But not even Herb fully appreciated the odds against him, even with McDonald's support. Even back in the 1970s, thousands of food products were launched and abandoned every year in the United States alone (today, that number is approximately 20,000 annually). About 80 percent failed because of flaws in consumer research, product placement, overpricing or misdirected advertising.

Often companies misread their customers. Pepsi's completely colorless Crystal Pepsi was supposed to seem pure as water, but customers didn't take to a cola that just didn't look like one. Herb's friend Oscar Mayer introduced his customers to Frank'n Stuff, a hot dog filled with chunks of cheese and chili. But so few people like cheese on their hot dogs that Frank'n Stuff didn't survive long enough to become infamous. The same fate befell Kellogg's Breakfast Mates, a box of cereal containing milk that didn't require refrigeration. Although warm, unrefrigerated milk is popular in Europe,

American parents never came to accept it. So Breakfast Mates, Frank'n Stuff and Crystal Pepsi joined the long list of food-product flops.

Ray Kroc's support provided a critical advantage, but Herb knew it was only the beginning. There were many other people beyond Ray who needed convincing.

At Ray's urging, Herb prepared to take his campaign to Chicago.

One morning, his wife, Barbara, watched as Herb packed for the trip. She suppressed her mirth as she watched him open an elegant attaché case and fill it, carefully, with a box of Bays English muffins, a stack of cheese, slices of round-cut bacon and a couple of ice packs. He added some nicely folded napkins and an iron cooking ring. He clicked the case shut like a culinary James Bond. He was off to cook the second most important breakfast of his life. Barbara hoped no one would inspect his luggage—or smell it!

The January snowstorm that greeted him in Chicago didn't diminish his enthusiasm. He took a taxi to the home of an old friend, where he cooked through a dry run of his presentation for an audience of one. Not until he felt ready did he turn in—and dream of eggs.

THE YOLK OF THE MATTER

Be conscientious about your "objectors."

10

PUT ON A SHOW

The white, eight-story McDonald's headquarters in Oak Brook, Illinois, seemed to rise straight out of the surrounding snow when Herb approached the main entrance the next morning. He walked into the gleaming stainless steel test kitchen to face an audience of about half a dozen men. A couple were food-safety experts who could barely conceal their displeasure at having to entertain another brainstorm from yet another franchisee. They all wore stony expressions. Ever since Jim Delligatti's success with the Big Mac and Lou Groen's with the Filet-O-Fish, restaurant operators like Herb had inundated them with ideas for new dishes. Most they rejected out of hand.

McDonald's president Fred Turner was there, too, and he was staunchly predisposed to dislike Herb's idea even before he saw it. "We are in the fast-growth, limited-menu business," Fred liked to say. The speed and success of McDonald's awe-inspiring expansion depended largely upon the simplicity of its menu. Adding new items meant increasing inventory, expenses and complexity. In short, it posed a big risk.

"If Fred was negative about it, it wouldn't have gone anyplace," remembered Paul Schrage, McDonald's Executive Vice President and marketing chief, who was among those gathered that day. Ray was also there, and that gave Herb real confidence.

As he grew older, Ray had begun turning over day-to-day management of his big and growing company to Fred, who had served as a counter and grill man in Ray's first restaurant and written its first operations and training manual. Ray and Fred liked to spend time together flying in prop planes over growing suburban communities, counting church steeples as they did. The more spires, they decided, the more reason to open a new restaurant in that city or town. As Ray spent more of his time in California, overseeing the West Coast operations of the company, he left the rest to Fred. "The rest" was a lot. It included all of the East Coast, the Midwest, the South and Canada.

Born showmen like Herb are accustomed to facing difficult crowds. Herb could muster enough courage to walk on stage and sing for thousands or even carry a machine gun into the surf under fire from the enemy. No one's life hung in the balance that day in the test kitchen, but the stakes were high enough that Herb's neatly pressed shirt was already wet with perspiration underneath his jacket. He hoped no one could tell that he was sweating more than he had on those mornings at the grill trying and failing to make the perfect sandwich. After so much preparation, now, it had come down to this moment.

Snapping open his leather attaché case, he began carefully removing a series of implements, one-by-one, including spatulas and his tailor-made egg ring. "I have always loved eggs benedict," he began. "And so one day I was thinking, What could we do to expand our business?" Herb had been practicing these moves at great lengths. Al Golin, the head of McDonald's longtime public relations agency, Golin Harris, could feel the tension in the room at the prospect of this radical change. "Herb, this has to be the most formal food presentation I've ever seen," he teased. But Herb didn't break character, sensing the moment called for an exacting performance. Above all, he needed to concentrate his persuasive powers on Fred, a manager so obsessive about operational matters that he was prone to calling people at 2 a.m. to discuss them.

Herb set the iron egg ring on the already hot grill and emptied a succession of eggs into it. "This is the answer to a real consumer need," he said, "and it will lend McDonald's a touch of class." He split several Bays English muffins in two and dropped them in the toaster. He laid slices of round-cut bacon on the grill next to the eggs and unwrapped slices of cheese, which he set aside at the ready. Looking up from the grill, he told the onlookers about the enduring appeal of eggs benedict and why this version—"the poor man's eggs benedict," as he called it—would prove the perfect solution to the breakfast problem.

As they watched, a couple of the onlookers discovered they felt hungry despite their misgivings about everything this test meal represented. As Herb finished each one, he placed the muffin halves side by side just like eggs benedict. "This way, people can eat one side of the muffin with jelly," Ray pointed out enthusiastically. No, a couple of the other men said, it should be served so that you could hold it in one hand. A debate then ensued over the best way to serve Herb's creation as he handed out a half dozen of them.

Finally, Herb cleared his throat.

"Gentlemen," he said, as everyone around him chewed his creation. "I propose we call this our 'Fast Break Break-Fast.'"

THE YOLK OF THE MATTER

If you're going to be the star,
make sure you know your lines.

11

PLAY THE NAME GAME
TO WIN

A s they finished their sandwiches, the small audience of a half dozen milled about talking. Fred Turner, who had been known to simply walk out of food demonstrations, was still there. So were the other members of the test audience, who devoured every sandwich Herb made. Even Fred ate one. Everyone had to admit they were delicious and that their compact size was smart. All of Herb's extensive experimentation and research had paid off. Many years later, Fred would recall that the specifications of Herb's first sandwich were so appealing, so inherently right, that they hardly changed over the following years. In fact, the very first sandwiches Herb served in that test kitchen were almost exactly the same as those eventually gobbled up by 210 million Americans a year.

The name, however, was another matter.

Everyone at the meeting, Ray included, liked "Fast Break Break-Fast." Herb, the eternal ad man, had done it again. "I loved that line. I wanted to use it," Paul Schrage, the marketing chief, recalled. Smart and catchy, the name said "convenience," which everyone knew was particularly important to the people who ate at their restaurants. It was fun to say, too, even if it was a little long.

But when the matter went to the company's lawyers, they discovered someone had already claimed the name as their own. That somebody was another company called Nabisco. As it happened, Nabisco never used the name—and to this day, still hasn't—but it was legally theirs if they wanted it. The world would never know Herb's clever word play because someone had beaten him to it.

Still, Herb returned home to Santa Barbara jubilant. McDonald's had decided to give his breakfast sandwich a try. Work began on procuring supplies nationwide, testing marketing ideas and introducing the concept to other owner-operators. Herb continued to serve his creation to more and more customers, calling it by his catchy name until someone came up with something else. Just as he had once experimented with the sandwich itself, he now began experimenting with new names, asking people's advice at home and at work. But nothing stuck.

Six months after Herb's triumph at the company headquarters, Ray and Fred and their wives happened to go out to dinner back in Chicago. It was a chilly night when they sat down in the restaurant at the Ambassador East Hotel, a haunt of celebrities and city politicos. They slipped into Ray's favorite booth and ordered drinks, talking about the usual mix of business and domestic events. When the subject of this new breakfast sandwich came up, the evening was in full swing.

It was either Fred or his wife who came up with the name first. The question of which one would become a point of good-natured rivalry between the two. Fred said he did, but Patty said, no, *she* did. But one of them had definitely uttered the words "Egg McMuffin." Ray would set the matter to rest years later at a companywide meeting. Introducing Patty before the assembly, Ray told everyone she was the one who had coined the name of the sandwich that would become so important to each and every one of them. As Ray made the announcement, Fred sat there next to his wife, smiling. "Keep quiet, dummy," he told himself. He knew that no matter who got credit, this clever play on the company name, McDonald's, was going to be good for everyone. It would also be the first of many Mc-based names on the menu in the restaurant company's long history, the progenitor of Chicken McNuggets, McFlurry dessert and McCafé years later.

That night at dinner in Chicago, they toasted the Egg McMuffin. Now it was just a matter of spreading the word.

THE YOLK OF THE MATTER

Fall in love with the first name if you must,
but marry the one that will last forever.

12

GENTLEMEN, START YOUR GRILLS!

How many brilliant ideas flounder in the execution? It's impossible to say, of course, but the answer is surely hundreds, thousands, maybe even millions times the number that actually succeed. For Herb's breakfast sandwich to catch fire, so many things still needed to happen.

Already so many improbable events had lined up in its favor. First, Herb took his own idea seriously when it occurred to him to make a tidy meal out of its elegant, but messy, inspiration. Then he mustered the resolve to follow the idea through. Next, despite a marked inability to cook, he'd managed to come up with something irresistible. Certainly, his relationship with Ray was crucial, but that was still just one essential element. Every day Ray turned down new ideas from his franchisees. Whoever thought up this solution to the problem of breakfast needed to have Herb's buoyancy and his persuasive personality.

The changes that still needed to happen remained largely beyond Herb's control. Company leaders needed to convince all the people who ran the restaurants out there that the Egg McMuffin would be good for them. This happened over the course of a couple of years during companywide meetings and countless communications.

In 1975, McDonald's launched its solution to the breakfast problem nationwide with an advertising campaign centered entirely around Herb's creation: "Introducing the Egg McMuffin. Everything you love for breakfast. In a sandwich."

But the result was underwhelming. It turned out that offering just one meal for breakfast didn't provide enough variety to drive traffic from repeat customers.

This was frustrating—so much so that Fred even considered abandoning Herb's idea. Franchisees everywhere had started opening up their doors at 7 a.m. with a worker at the grill and another at the window only to sell two or three Egg McMuffins all morning. They were losing money—and confidence.

Ken Lopaty, who ran dozens of restaurants with his brother in California and elsewhere, visited headquarters about this time. "Well, we can just drop it," Fred said to Ken as they discussed the disappointing debut.

"Fred, we're not dropping it," Ken responded. "The only reason we're not selling more is we don't have variety. People will come in for breakfast twice a week if we give them more options." Given enough time, Ken was convinced breakfast at McDonald's, including the Egg McMuffin, would eventually hit. It took McDonald's about six months to figure out that only a full breakfast menu would build the kind of traffic they wanted. First, the company added a Danish, orange juice and hot cakes. Next came scrambled eggs, sausages and hash browns. All the while, McDonald's kept up its advertising campaign—one that has never really stopped in all the decades that followed. Because it was the best brand, a dish unique to McDonald's with the catchiest name, the Egg McMuffin featured prominently in the new ads, including one with this line: "McDonald's introduces some breakfasts like Mom used to make. Plus one she didn't." The Egg McMuffin acted like an engine that pulled the rest of breakfast train behind it.

"Thank God Fred went along with it," Ken said. "I shudder to think where we'd be today without breakfast."

Suddenly people were coming to work at McDonald's at 4:30 a.m. instead of 8 a.m. Opening up much earlier in the morning meant each restaurant had to hire more people. They had to change the way their schedules operated.

In the meantime, untold quantities of muffins, eggs and ham began to be produced on a regular basis, putting bakeries, egg producers and bacon suppliers into overdrive. At first this meant a great boon for Bays as McDonald's launched the Egg McMuffin using only Herb's favorite English muffins. "All of a sudden everyone across the country was tasting our English muffins and, pretty soon, they weren't as exotic as they had been," said James N. Bay, grandson of the company's founder. Years later, McDonald's reached far and wide for other suppliers, becoming one of the world's largest consumers of eggs and of English muffins.

Back in Santa Barbara, the revenue from breakfast helped improve Herb's personal income. Things went so well that he opened another restaurant and then another. Between 1968 and 1999, he and his son, David, would open a total of six restaurants— four in Santa Barbara and two in the neighboring town of Goleta. But even as Herb's small restaurant empire expanded, he clung to the same principle of taking care of other people that led him to dream up the increasingly popular Egg McMuffin. He knew he wasn't just in the restaurant business. You could say he had a much deeper mission in life.

THE YOLK OF THE MATTER

Hold tight til it's right,
and then let it go to watch it grow.

13

BUY THE ELEPHANT

Herb's creation, the Egg McMuffin, did exactly what he hoped it would: it solved the problem with breakfast in Santa Barbara, California. And with all of McDonald's behind it, it was on its way to doing the same throughout the country. It also brought in the extra income that enabled Herb to take care of his family and many hungry people at his growing number of restaurants.

It also did something else. It turned Herb into somewhat of a star—a local star, of course, but a star nonetheless. It was just enough celebrityhood for Herb. For someone who always loved to perform, this was truly wonderful. In Herb's view, life was meant to be lived to the fullest. He understood that not everyone could grow up to perform in movies or on the stage. But that didn't mean they couldn't live with great spirit, that they couldn't star in their own lives and in their own communities. Having achieved a small bit of acclaim, Herb wanted to share it. He wanted to imbue the lives of those around him with laughter, wonder and excitement.

Which is why he decided to buy an elephant.

Herb particularly enjoyed the moment when he walked into the local bank, sat down with the manager and said, "I need to borrow $3,500. To buy an elephant."

The manager didn't know what to say at first. It was one of the more unusual requests the bank had ever entertained, but nonetheless, the answer came back yes.

As he had done with eggs benedict, Herb had fallen in love with the small Santa

Barbara Zoo. His elephant adventure began the day he called the zoo director, Ted McToldridge, to ask if there was anything the zoo needed. Herb was thinking of perhaps one small wallaby, a diminutive relative of the kangaroo. Wallabies had captured Herb's imagination when he passed through Australia during his military service.

"I don't need a wallaby, Herb," Ted told Herb, halting his reverie. "I need an elephant!"

Before long, a baby Asian elephant was delivered all the way from India, as a gift for the entire community, to expand the zoo which, at the time, was only slightly larger than a petting zoo.

Eventually, the zoo would have two elephants from Herb and the local insurance company that underwrote their passage. They were named Little Mac and Sujatha. More than forty years later, they are still there for everyone to see, full grown and munching on stacks of hay under the bright Californian sun.

Even though Herb was known for his restaurants in Santa Barbara, he was still a newcomer from Chicago. He wanted to be part of the community upon which he and his restaurants depended. Herb wanted to make a mark on his community personally and on behalf of his business. And he wanted to do something that would bring wonder and delight to the lives of the people in that community, whether it was solving the problem with breakfast or enabling the zoo to bring elephants to town as its newest honorable citizens.

His company, McDonald's, urged all of its restaurant operators to give back to their communities whenever possible. In fact, it more than urged them; it demanded as much. This directive came from Ray who often said, "None of us is as good as all of us." The company taught its operators that community investment was the essence of McDonald's. This made great sense, of course. As of 2007, McDonald's had invested a collective total of $28 billion in its communities in the United States alone just in the course of conducting its business. To ensure those communities stayed healthy, franchisees also donated to local causes and charities.

For Herb, this duty was more than simply a financial investment; it was an investment in his soul. He sat on the zoo's board of directors longer than anybody in its history at that time and served as its board president. Herb also helped found the zoo's zoological society and for many years, his wife, Barbara, managed the zoo's gift shop as a volunteer.

Herb and his son, David, donated food and modest sums of money to dozens and dozens of charities every year. To raise money for schools, they would invite local teachers to work behind the counters in the evenings all week long and to take home

20 percent of that week's profits. They collected Christmas presents for needy local children. They put out coin boxes that attracted several thousand dollars every year for a local food bank. They took note of the fact that the hospital in town was too small to justify a full Ronald McDonald House, where families stay for free while their ailing children receive treatment at nearby hospitals. So Herb convinced McDonald's to provide a sizable grant to help build a small cottage in town that would serve the same purpose. Herb and David donated food to parent-teacher associations, Cub Scout troops, youth soccer leagues and many sporting events for kids and adults. They contributed to research to help cure diseases like muscular dystrophy and Alzheimer's. The list went—and still goes—on and on and on.

Herb believed, as his son still does, in paying it forward, and that taking care of others would come back to them in more ways than they could imagine.

∞ ∞ ∞

It took Herb a couple of years to pay back the bank for the loan that purchased the elephants. In honor of Ray Kroc's birthday, his brother Bob gave the zoo a donation that paid for the elephants' enclosure and upkeep for many more years. Decades later, that investment continued to pay dividends for the people of the town, for the company Herb founded and for Herb. Every year, Herb's restaurants threw their own party on zoo grounds, and everyone who came delighted in the elephants. Herb always made sure there were plenty of Egg McMuffins on hand to mark the occasion.

THE YOLK OF THE MATTER

The restaurant business doesn't just serve food, but also people.

14

HIRE THE HARPIST

At home in Santa Barbara, as Herb's own company continued to grow, some people thought Herb gave away more Egg McMuffins than he actually sold. That was a *slight* exaggeration, but Herb did feel life was too short to hold back on giving and celebrating life with others. He wanted to share the solution to the breakfast problem with as many people as possible. He kept coupons for free Egg McMuffins in the breast pocket of his jacket. He handed them out to anyone and everyone he encountered. They became his calling card.

His admirers came to include chefs who specialized in haute cuisine, like Julia Child. A neighbor in town, Julia became a good friend of Herb. In fact, the doyenne of French cuisine secretly loved McDonald's French fries. Although she never gave in, Herb, who remained an adman at heart, couldn't resist asking her to appear in at least one McDonald's commercial. At her eightieth birthday, Julia was fêted by the best chefs from around the world. Herb was there, too. Given that he had always tried to bring five-star quality to his restaurants, Herb felt delighted to be in their company. The day he met Wolfgang Puck, the celebrated chef asked Herb how he himself could invent a meal as successful as the Egg McMuffin. Stick with simple and irresistible, Herb suggested. Then, for good measure, he gave Wolfgang coupons for free Egg McMuffins.

Herb didn't restrict his food giveaways to the Egg McMuffin. By this time, he and David were running their company along with Monte Fraker, who had first come to work for Herb when he was sixteen and, more than thirty years later, was Herb's director of operations and close family friend. Every year, Herb's restaurants gave out free apple pies to all the teachers in town on the first day of school. Whenever wildfires broke out and threatened homes in the hills of the town, Herb, David and Monte gave away thousands of free meals to the men and women who braved great danger to fight them. All of this giving was done for the community that had given so much to Herb, his family, his restaurants and all the people who worked there.

Herb focused on a special segment of his community every November 10, the anniversary of the U.S. Marines, by offering free Big Macs to U.S. Marines or Marine veterans. All they had to do was show him their military ID. Or they could show him a tattoo. Or they could just sing. Herb liked to break into the U.S. Marine anthem when he met another Marine. Often he and his new friend would sing, loudly and proudly, right there in the center of the restaurant, stopping onlookers in their tracks. It brought tears to Herb's eyes.

Herb's feelings about his military service ran deep. During World War II, he fought throughout the Pacific, including Okinawa. He served in the First Marines division that lost nearly 60 percent of its men on the island of Peleliu, site of the infamous battle with the highest casualty rate in the Pacific during the war. He didn't talk too much about the men he knew who lost their lives on Peleliu or elsewhere, but his friends and family knew those experiences lived inside him. Herb understood he was a very, *very* lucky man. He never lost sight of that fact, even though he kept many of his war stories to himself.

Sometimes, just sitting at the table in his home kitchen, he'd look out the window at the garden and say, "Aren't we lucky to be living on this planet?" Or on holidays, he would sit quietly with a smile on his face as his grandkids hooted and hollered around the house. He'd glance at all of them and say, "Look at the fruit of my loins." This embarrassed them, and they rolled their eyes. "Bebop," they'd say, smiling, "that's kind of gross." But they were proud, too, to be part of the Peterson clan. Herb's eldest granddaughter, Beth, had started calling Herb "Bebop" as a toddler when she couldn't pronounce "grandpa," and the nickname stuck. Eventually, all of his ten other grandchildren called him Bebop, too. "Bebop" suited his spirit and sounded like something he might sing.

Herb knew how to turn family gatherings into memorable occasions. Every time the whole extended family got together, he stashed fifty crisp one-dollar bills in his breast pocket. When a grandchild carried out the trash, brought their grandmother something to drink, helped clear the table or helped wash the dishes, he handed them one. This freed the grown-ups for a more relaxed gathering, turning chores into a game for the kids and teaching them a little about enterprise at the same time.

After everyone sat down to eat, Herb always offered a toast, but rarely got through any of them. When moved by something, he cried as easily as he laughed.

As time went on, Herb kept up the tradition of surprising and delighting his customers. David and Monte picked up on this tradition. They hired a harpist to play inside his restaurants downtown. They also brought in pianists, gospel singers and, once, a group of break-dancers. When it started raining, Herb ushered the dancers inside to perform. Another time, to the delight of kids, they brought in a band of charismatic octogenarians who played kazoos. Sometimes David went overboard. A one-man band played so loud that the music drowned out every other sound in the restaurant and sent customers fleeing. Herb just laughed.

Herb kept watering his fresh pots of yellow mums, tending to them as if they were children. When it came time to bring in new ones, his customers went home with pots of the flowers to take home and plant in their gardens.

THE YOLK OF THE MATTER

Share the eggs in your basket.

15

CHANGE THE WORLD
ONE SMILE AT A TIME

Every day, Herb practiced his belief that he could change the world one smile at a time. The more smiles he coaxed out of people in a day, the better. He might do this by offering them a free Egg McMuffin or simply opening a door for them. David grew up watching his father and learning from him. Because Herb was a father figure to him, Monte Fraker did, too, as did many other people in the company.

Like Herb, David understood that the family business was about much more than serving food. It was really about taking care of people and making them happy. From time to time, someone would learn just how many resources Herb and David invested every year in the people who worked with them, as well as in the community, and that person would say, "Just run your company like a business!" And David would respond, "Well, we can't! It's not just a business to us. It's a family." Herb, David and Monte knew that, in order to take care of their customers, they had to take care of the people who worked for them first.

This was a challenging task, even more so than solving the problem with breakfast. In Herb and David's industry, annual employee turnover could be very high—as much as 200 percent or more. That meant that, over the course of a year, a competing restaurant might have to hire two or three people to fill one job opening because so many people would leave for different opportunities. David understood why. The work was fast-paced and sometimes exhausting. Serving an endless stream of hungry people, like any job anywhere, could become overwhelming if a company allowed that to happen. "It could wipe you out if you don't put a spirit of fun into it," David said. So Herb, David and Monte came up with inventive ways to inject their restaurants with humanity and life.

They held contests every year to see which restaurant could meet the target for the fastest and friendliest service or the cleanest bathrooms. The latter came to be known as "Operation Urinal" and had one and only goal: keep it clean! Winners received tickets to Disneyland and Dodgers games. The three men threw themselves into companywide contests in these same areas, taking top honors in their region and throughout the land. Winning contest prizes became a source of giddy, cloak-and-dagger adventure when David and Monte posted sentries on the roofs of their restaurants. Peering through binoculars, the lookouts tried to spot undercover "mystery shoppers" sent by McDonald's to measure their performance.

Throughout the year, they also held events like softball or volleyball tournaments and company picnics. When restaurant team members graduated from being green-card holders to U.S. citizens, Herb and David honored them before everyone else in the company by giving them commemorative plaques. They threw baby showers for team members who became pregnant so those mothers-to-be could go home with a carload full of diapers, clothing and other necessaries. Every year, Monte took ten managers at a time on camping trips to places like Yosemite and Big Sur, giving them four uninterrupted days to hike and bond without the distraction of email or television. Herb, who used to take his whole family camping, understood the power of getting out into the wild together. He and David paid for all those trips and happily scrambled to fill the missing hours those managers left in the work schedules. There was always a long waiting list of managers wanting to go.

Every year during the Christmas season, Herb, David and Monte decorated an old fire truck for the local holiday parade. People who worked at the restaurants donned bright red sweaters bearing the company name and rode proudly through town with Ronald McDonald, who was a constant fixture in the community. Herb led everybody on board in Christmas carols. Being a part of the holiday parade was such a simple thing, really, but it gave everyone a sense of belonging.

David, Herb and Monte got to know the people who worked with them, as well as their employees' family members.

But, although all these things were nice, they still weren't enough. They knew they needed to do even more.

∞ ∞ ∞

After working alongside Herb and learning from him for many years, David and Monte began to feel they were operating more than a restaurant company; they were running a ministry of sorts. Herb even dubbed one of their team members "the Chaplain."

Agustin DeGuevara, who is now eighty-six, worked for much of his career as a manager at Santa Barbara's luxurious Biltmore Hotel. When he turned sixty-four, on a dare from a friend, he took a job at McDonald's, never imagining he'd stay for more than two decades. Born in the coastal city of San Sebastian, in the Basque part of Spain, Agustin was raised in orphanages in Mexico. After coming to the United States, he worked in the fields alongside other immigrants before climbing the ranks at the Biltmore. Refined, with an old world air, he wore Basque berets or Panama hats. He viewed his time with McDonald's less as a job and more as an opportunity to gently minister to people. That's how he earned his nickname, used first by Herb, then by everyone else.

"Anytime there was an emotional conflict, they sent the people involved to me," Agustin said. The Chaplain spent only a few years managing the restaurants and eventually graduated to serving as a host during peak meal times, greeting customers and opening doors for them. Even today, almost every day, the Chaplain sits down with his Bible at a table at the Milpas Street restaurant and waits. People from the company come to sit and talk about marriage, money or other life troubles.

Once, in a very sad turn of events, a longtime manager was discovered to have stolen money from the company. He lost his job over it, but not his connection to his former employers. David and Monte prayed with him and, often, the manager went to sit with Agustin DeGuevara, whom he'd known for decades, for his unique counsel and more prayer. "Agustin is a wise old sage," David said. "There's something about him, about an older man, that you can become transparent to."

∞ ∞ ∞

As the size of the staff at all their restaurants grew, David and Monte knew they needed to do more than just encourage their team members to talk about their problems. They needed solutions. Sometimes the problem was that one of their team members' children needed emergency dental work or someone else's home flooded after a pipe burst. On one occasion, a woman who worked for them found herself caught in an abusive relationship. Right there in the parking lot of one of the restaurants, her angry boyfriend tried to roughly push her into his car. An assistant manager rushed outside and helped her get away. Then she needed a place to stay for while getting back on her feet.

Sometimes there were so many needs like this that they could be a little overwhelming. So David and Monte came up with a unique solution. They created a nonprofit charity designed for the sole purpose of helping their people through crises. Every two weeks, the managers who wanted to (and most did) started donating small sums from every paycheck to a fund. From the moment David and Monte shared this idea with Herb, he liked it so much that he decided to personally match all the contributions the managers put in. It didn't take long for the balance in that fund to reach several thousand dollars.

When team members went through crises, they could bring their situations to their managers. Once a manager became convinced a team member had a problem the fund should address, he or she brought the matter to the company members on the board of the charity, who talked it over and took a vote. Ninety percent of the time, the board voted to use money in the fund to help solve the problem. "Our motto is 'give it away,'" Monte said. Every year a different manager ran the fund, and everyone involved learned a lot about the power of giving.

In this way, Herb, David and Monte and their company devised a mechanism to enable workers to pay for their children's dental surgeries, for emergency plumbing, or for a few months of rent. They called this charity their Helping Hand Fund, the idea being that sometimes a little help is all that's needed to get through a tough spot.

That's what happened to the woman in the abusive relationship. Years later, she was with a new man, expecting a baby and still working at McDonald's Santa Barbara.

THE YOLK OF THE MATTER

Your work is your ministry. Put your heart at the center of it.

16

TRUST THE INVISIBLE

Herb, David and Monte believed in several ideas and principles, which you couldn't always see or put your hands on, as you can a dollar bill or a basket of eggs. They wanted the people who worked with them to put stock in these concepts, too.

These ideas and principles are related to Herb's conviction that he could create something out of nothing—that from seemingly little, much good could be generated. David called this idea "trusting the invisible."

A former team member, Dan Deeble, who worked with Herb and David experienced it firsthand once when he bought a large trophy case for the company. By accident he bought the wrong one. It was a mistake that couldn't be undone, and it would cost the company $350. Dan swallowed hard before he brought the unfortunate news to David.

David listened as Dan spoke. He knew how smart and capable Dan typically was.

"Hey, we all make mistakes," David said, in response to Dan's admission. Then he quoted him a line from the company's Statement of Values: "(We) allow each other the room to stumble as well as the opportunity to succeed."

Matter resolved. Dan felt relief wash over him. He also felt deeply impressed. The experience made a lasting impression on him. He went back to work with new resolve.

David and Herb knew that in order to succeed, they needed to allow people to be human and imperfect. After all, if Herb hadn't allowed himself to make mistakes in the evolution of the Egg McMuffin, people would still be knocking on his door in the morning, begging for breakfast.

"This is a value you don't always see at work with your own eyes," David said, "but you feel it as powerfully as the sun on your face when you are in an environment that keeps it alive."

The Petersons and Monte worked with their managers, and with other people at their company, to write up an official Statement of Values. It went like this:

We take pride in offering our guests extraordinary service, fast and friendly, in a natural way. We will serve only the highest quality products in immaculate surroundings, all at a great value. We feel blessed to be part of this special community and are constantly seeking ways to return to it a part of our good fortune.

Our priority is people, aware that satisfied guests come from having satisfied coworkers. We recognize our role to build character and values that please God first. Our McDonald's family cares about matters of the heart: honesty, loyalty, respect, joy, patience and love. We build our family on these virtues, understanding that the most important aspects of life are not always visible.

We strive for balanced and healthy lives where we can prosper creatively, intellectually, financially and spiritually. We will teach and listen, allow each the room to stumble as well as the opportunity to succeed.

We are individuals working for a common purpose, not pushed by problems but led by dreams.

We are McDonald's Santa Barbara and Goleta.

All fine words, but the three knew the words were worth nothing if they weren't put into action every day. The three men were well aware that their high-minded Statement of Values could easily become just another piece of paper that hung, unimplemented, on the walls of their restaurants. So they took steps to make sure that would never happen.

At company meetings, they set the statement to music. Once Dan Deeble sang it with a goofy western twang as he strummed a guitar. They turned it into a skit. They engraved it on brass plaques and hung it where customers could see it in every restaurant.

They also talked about these values, often and enthusiastically, both in casual conversations, like the one between David and Dan, and in meetings. David made a standing offer to any team member: he would pay $100 to anyone who could recite it from memory.

The Statement of Values had a real impact on people like Dan and a manager named Marco Gavilanes, who came to work with Herb and David after nearly a decade at a big national competitor.

THE YOLK OF THE MATTER

Nothing's more valuable than your values.

17

SHOOT THE CONFETTI GUN

Herb and David had watched Marco Gavilanes for several years. Like all good business people, they frequented their local competition. Sometimes they discovered wonderful people who worked there—people like Marco.

Marco grew up in town and spent nine years at another national restaurant company in Santa Barbara. He wasn't sure he wanted to make the jump to McDonald's. In fact, the only opening there was at a lower salary. But he liked Herb and David. His own company hadn't expended much energy to inspire loyalty in him. His passion for work was generated entirely on his own. Eventually, Marco decided to give Herb and David a chance.

Marco's first day at McDonald's Santa Barbara happened to coincide with the State of the Onion, the annual meeting of the company's leadership, which included all the restaurant managers. That year it was held at the old adobe Santa Barbara Historical Museum. When he arrived, Marco was astonished to find himself enthusiastically introduced to the two dozen people there.

Then David, dressed like a clown, shot off a huge confetti gun to get the meeting underway. Watching the shredded paper rain down around him, Marco noticed there were dollar bills mixed in there, too—a lot of them. It was a piñata for adults (and David's way of upping the ante on his father's dollar-bill giveaway at family holiday parties). Marco grabbed about forty dollars and realized he was going to have to stay on his toes with this crowd.

Those weren't the only surprises of the day.

Marco thought he knew what to expect from annual company meetings. At his old company, the meetings were devoted to a review of the numbers. How did we do this year compared to last? How did our performance stack up to the goals we set out for ourselves? What are our goals for the upcoming year? It all boiled down to numbers, numbers, numbers.

But David and Monte teamed up to talk about the company's Statement of Values and their Twenty Basics, or basic codes of conduct the company expected of every manager. Herb, who by this time was in his early eighties, sat in the back, the grinning patriarch.

At David's urging, a manager stood up and said he had taken to heart one basic that stipulates that when disagreements crop up, they should be followed quickly by apologies and resolved before the end of the day. "I've started doing this at home with my parents," the manager said. "It's completely changed my life."

Then, at Monte's behest, a couple other managers who had never spoken publicly, and certainly not about anything personal, stood up and began to talk about when they had observed other managers putting some of the company's core values into action.

"Every time we do this, it makes us cry. We can't help it," David said. "By three in the afternoon we haven't even gotten to the numbers yet, all we're talking about is love, family and heartfelt things." Herb was so moved by these stories that he cried more than anyone.

Occasionally, the room fell silent. More often, everyone was laughing. It was more like a church retreat or an encounter group. Eventually the focus turned to numbers, but only briefly. Very quickly, Marco got to know people on a much deeper level than he had ever known anyone at his old company where, after almost ten years, nobody even knew the name of his girlfriend. On the first day with this new company, a few people already knew her name. When he and his girlfriend got married seven months later and their florist fell through at the last moment, Monte fronted Marco $1,000 to hire a replacement. When Marco and his wife bought their first house, David loaned him $20,000 on a handshake.

Marco began to notice that the company was filled with people who had started washing windows or working behind the register, and decades later were still there. These people included Monte and Harry Fountain, who McDonald's once named in the top 1 percent of all store managers in the nation. Harry had been with the company almost twenty-five years. Bonifacio Sixto, or Boni, as everyone calls him, had eighteen years with the company and Omar Santos more than ten. Of the 250 people in the company, 20 had been there ten years or longer, 16 had been there for fifteen years, and 2 had been there for nearly thirty years. In fact, many of these people worked alongside their parents, children, siblings and spouses. As Omar Santos said, "We're building a McFamily here."

"You are here to learn as much as you can," David said to everyone who joined the company. When teaching managers how to treat their coworkers, Monte told them, "You may be one of the only parents some people have."

Eventually Monte challenged Marco to extend some of this care even to the most difficult customers at the stores he managed. In response, Marco befriended some of the homeless people who frequented the Milpas Street location. He kept up a relationship with a man named Joe even after Joe had fallen off the wagon yet again. One day before checking back in to rehab, Joe stopped by to thank Marco for the kindness he'd shown him.

Experiences like this one and riding on the McDonald's fire truck with his family in the annual holiday parade made Marco feel, for the first time, that he'd become a true member of the community he'd grown up in.

∞ ∞ ∞

As the fire truck and confetti gun suggest, the Petersons' McDonald's team members were a family that made a point of having fun together—just as Herb always did with his extended biological family every time they gathered for vacations or family holidays (and for the Peterson family, even small holidays like St. Patrick's Day were occasions to dress up and celebrate together). In the main offices at McDonald's Santa Barbara you'll find a drawer filled with some unusual items that help the Petersons' McFamily have fun at work: head-to-toe regalia for several species of clown costumes, cheerleader uniforms, walking canes, hats and wigs of every imaginable color and hairstyle. At McDonald's Santa Barbara, you never know when that drawer will come in handy.

When aiming for a new high watermark in company sales, David and Monte once turned up at the managers' meeting dressed as cheerleaders with pom-poms to cheer the troops on. Depending on the theme or scene, Herb might have shown up as a pirate, a safari guide, a seventies dude in a huge 'fro or any other get-up—the more absurd the better. For some reason, no one nodded off during these meetings.

The costume drawer also came in handy when shooting training videos, in which David and Monte starred and Herb made cameos. In a what-not-to-do kitchen safety video, Monte suddenly lost his head in a particularly nasty cooking accident. Blood (actually ketchup) sprayed all over everything in sight. Dressed up as hippies and old codgers who were hard of hearing, David and Monte acted out the roles of impossible customers. One year, wearing a fake balding pate and full safari gear, Monte spoofed the man everyone affectionately called Mr. P.

Always the showman, Herb delighted in the theatrics. Why hold a typical meeting, Herb, David and Monte figured, when you can create a memorable experience everyone will talk about for years to come? Some companies view their restaurant locations as islands that do not interact with one another. At McDonald's Santa Barbara, everyone from all the different restaurants knows each other and, instinctively, helps each other out, with or without the knowledge or involvement of the company management. "It's amazing," Monte said.

It wouldn't be Herb's company if, despite the shenanigans, the meeting didn't begin with a full pledge of allegiance and everyone joining in to sing "The Star Spangled Banner." Often quite a few newcomers to the company found themselves singing it for the first time. At McDonald's Santa Barbara it's OK to be a bleeding heart—and a goofball.

∞ ∞ ∞

David and Monte wanted managers like Marco Gavilanes to know how important they were to the company. Once a year, David took all the managers on trips to shake things up and give them a different perspective on their work. They visited the famous Pike's Place fish market in Seattle and watched the world-famous fishmongers there turn drudge work into a fun and exciting daily performance. He took the managers to stay at the Four Seasons in San Francisco to soak up some of the best customer service the world has to offer. Once a year, David and Monte took managers like Marco shopping at Nordstrom's to pick out new wardrobes, consisting of several full outfits from shoes to slacks to coats.

At the company's annual Christmas party, the dress was formal. Men who wanted to came in tuxedos, which was Herb's favorite choice, unless he went with slacks in a Santa Claus or Christmas tree pattern. Women wore gowns, often ones purchased specially for the event. The point was to keep up the sartorial spirit set by Herb, who continued to come to work spiffed up even in his later years, when it took him longer to dress. By encouraging their people to look their best, David and Monte were urging them to bring their best to work every day. "Mr. P passed that on to us," said Marco. "The moment you walk in the restaurant or drive into the parking lot, you know you're on stage."

It was a message that resounded far beyond the borders of Santa Barbara.

THE YOLK OF THE MATTER

Hatch a batch of happiness.

18

LET IT RIPPLE

After almost forty years in business, David and Herb figured that close to 10,000 people had worked at their six restaurants. Despite the company's relatively low turnover, there was only so much room for upward advancement. For many people, McDonald's was their first experience in the working world.

When high school or college was over or when it was time for team members to move on, they did. What continually surprised Herb, David and Monte was how frequently they and their managers ran into former "McFamily members." It happened all the time.

One day Monte bumped into Cesar Medina, who worked with him nearly twenty years before for just five months, when Cesar was fifteen. Cesar had gone on to work as the safety manager of one of the county's largest trash and recycling companies, Marborg Industries. He told Monte, "If it wasn't for McDonald's, I don't think I would have had the skills I have now. I learned at a young age the values I needed to survive."

Like Cesar, many former family members have stories to tell about how they applied the work ethic, spirit and commitment to invisible values from McDonald's with great success elsewhere. They explained how they'd become better bankers, teachers, hairdressers and waste-management technicians. Some of their stories are eye-popping.

Michael McMillan, who worked with Herb back in the early days of the Egg McMuffin, went on to build a string of thirteen urgent-care medical centers just north of Santa Barbara. His company generates annual revenues six times those of his former employer's.

"Some of the things I learned at McDonald's are things I do here every day," Michael said. He marveled at the way McDonald's created a reliable, predictable experience for customers every time they came back. He decided that his company needed to do the same for basic medical services, from treating cuts to prescribing antibiotics. Other things he learned at McDonald's included counting and keeping track of everything from inventory to money, keeping the trash bins emptied and cleaning the equipment every night to a lustrous shine just as Michael had done years earlier with McDonald's grill. It included creating an environment that, while fast-paced and demanding, was also fun and engaging.

Dan Deeble was a recent graduate from the local college when he started working at McDonald's. Though he considered attending the seminary, Dan wondered whether he should stay at McDonald's after his first several months there. "Why become a pastor?" he thought. "Here is the living faith I've been looking for." But there just weren't enough good positions open for Dan to aspire to at Santa Barbara McDonald's. Reluctantly, he left. Dan's path ultimately took him all the way out to Overland Park, Kansas, where he became the lead pastor for a rapidly growing church. That title means he is responsible for the church's overall direction. Every Sunday he tries to apply the same creativity and care for people that he learned with the Petersons.

"I felt immensely loved there," Dan said, remembering the time Monte started paying him a commission after a program he oversaw began making a profit. "Gosh, they really took care of me."

How David and Herb had handled a botched trophy case had made all the difference in the world.

THE YOLK OF THE MATTER

*When you take care of people, they take care of you—
and many others, too.*

19

SAY GOODBYE WITH LOVE

Even as he closed in on ninety, Herb still kept coming to work, always dressed immaculately, always eager to talk to his customers and team members. He liked to pay all of his six restaurants a visit every day. Sometimes, however, it was all he could do to just drive over to one or two and spend some time in the parking lot, getting a feel for how things were going and waving to friends. Occasionally he took a nap there in his car with its locally famous EGG MC1 license plate, as people bustled in and out of their cars around him. People got used to seeing him out there with the motor running, taking a snooze.

Once a month or so, the company managers would grade each restaurant. Herb's reports came to be known, fondly, as "Herbie's Hundreds." He just couldn't seem to score any of the restaurants less than 100 percent. In his mind they all deserved A's. If any one got less than 100 percent from Herb something had to be really, *really* wrong.

As the years went on, Herb's memory began to fade. The smiles were less frequent on his usually cheery face. On the afternoon when Herb passed away, David was alone at his father's side, telling him how much he loved him. After Herb was gone, David took great pride and care in dressing his father in his favorite gray flannel slacks, tweed jacket and pink button-down shirt with a horizontally striped pink and gray tie.

More than six hundred people thronged the church for Herb's funeral.

Many of his former team members came. People flew in from around the country and around the world. David faced them all and played host to a rousing celebration of Herb's life.

Herb left behind thousands of people who loved him—a sprawling family clan, six thriving restaurants, roughly ten thousand former team members who'd learned from him. He also left a proud record of military service, two Asian elephants and the Egg McMuffin, a simple creation that stands as a testament to the power that one simple idea can generate.

His widow, Barbara, opened his closet to his eleven grandkids so they could take one or two of his colorful ties. They understood that they themselves were the products of their grandfather's constant dreaming. He began conjuring up dreams of his future grandchildren more than sixty years earlier as he wooed their grandmother through letters written during a horrible war, hoping he would live to see her again. And, like so many things in Herb's life, those dreams came true.

Of course, Egg McMuffins were served at the celebration following Herb's funeral. And before everyone said their final goodbyes, David placed an Egg McMuffin next to his father, very gently, before Herb was lowered into the ground.

THE *REAL* YOLK OF THE MATTER

Be a good egg.

EPILOGUE

ONE GOOD EGG LEADS TO ANOTHER

After Herb passed away, one of his friends came up with this little ditty:

> *There is more in the middle of the Egg McMuffin*
> *than an egg in the middle of the muffin.*
> *There's a little bit of Herb*
> *in every Egg McMuffin.*

In his final years, as his faculties slowly dimmed, Herb could no longer track the progress of his solution to the problem with breakfast. But by then, of course, the Egg McMuffin had more than taken on a life of its own and was destined to endure far beyond the lifespan of the man who created it.

None of the biggest competitors of McDonald's got around to serving breakfast until long after the Egg McMuffin made its debut. By then, McDonald's had firmly established its dominance in this market and today still holds a 30 percent share.

Breakfast and the Egg McMuffin were such a success, in fact, that over time, the first meal of the day would come to account for 20 to 30 percent of McDonald's revenues overall. This meant that if one restaurant brought in annual revenues of $2 million, $400,000 to $600,000 came from breakfast. Put more simply, for every dollar McDonald's brings in, about twenty-five cents comes from breakfast. Often that amount accounts almost exactly for the per-location advantage in annual sales that most McDonald's restaurants enjoy over their competitors.

Even though the Egg McMuffin debuted many decades ago, its ongoing impact is still being felt. If you add up 20 to 30 percent of McDonald's revenue from the 1970s until today, from billions and billions of customers in more than 30,000 restaurants worldwide, it goes without saying that this number would come to billions and billions of dollars.

And it all started with a palm-sized egg sandwich that still costs about what you pay for a cup of coffee.

∞ ∞ ∞

Herb was especially proud of one little known fact about the egg sandwich he created: it still is one of the healthiest items on his restaurants' menu. At just 300 calories, it's nutritious without being heavy.

Herb was also proud of the fact that David and his wife and three kids supply living proof that the Egg McMuffin could be part of a healthy lifestyle. They eat Egg McMuffins all the time, sometimes every day, and each one also happens to be a high-caliber athlete in at least one sport. David was a top tennis player in high school and still plays tennis and runs triathalons. His wife, Sue, was the fastest swimmer in the world in the fifty-yard freestyle in 1976 and 1977. She won her college championships and narrowly missed competing on the 1984 Olympic swimming team. David and Sue's eldest, daughter Whitney, played Division I tennis for USC and California Polytechnic State University. Their son, Parker, plays Division 1 water polo at Pepperdine. Their youngest, daughter Lakey, is a member of the USA Surf Team and was recently named the top female surfer in the country under age fourteen.

You'd be hard-pressed to find a more active bunch. After working out together in the morning, they often head out for Egg McMuffins. David is always trying to extend his passion for health and physical fitness to his family at work. He's hired personal trainers to help restaurant managers work out at local tracks. He's held fitness competitions at the company. And he makes sure McDonald's Santa Barbara supports countless sports teams for kids and adults in the community.

Herb—urged on by his wife, Barbara—always had a keen interest in healthy eating. He loved fresh foods. You could say he was a good-food junkie. He was so frustrated that the world did not see McDonald's as serving the highest quality food. "He just didn't understand it," David said. If he thought a change was afoot that might negatively alter the quality of McDonald's food, he would go on a tirade to stop it.

After the success of his Egg McMuffin, Herb set out to convince McDonald's to offer a variety of healthy meals. To help people lower their cholesterol levels, he tried, unsuccessfully, to persuade McDonald's to offer a yolk-free version of the Egg McMuffin to anyone who requested it. Next came fresh salads, introduced in the early 1980s. For a time, Herb sold a small salad in a cup with carrots that he dubbed McVeggies. Over a six-month trial period, Herb offered in his downtown restaurants a full salad bar where people served themselves heaping plates of fresh greens along with their burgers. The salad bar was popular, just not enough so to persuade McDonald's to take the idea national. Of course, today, McDonald's offers a full menu of fresh salads. These salads closely resemble sketches for prepackaged salads that Herb made back in the 1980s. "Dad was just a couple of decades ahead of his time," David said.

Right up until the end of his life, Herb was still enthusiastically developing a hearty oatmeal dish and trying to persuade everyone he worked with that it was as good an idea as the Egg McMuffin. Creating new products, designing their packaging and dreaming up new ways of marketing them kept Herb engaged and excited long after he'd turned the active management of the company over to his son.

∞ ∞ ∞

After the Egg McMuffin began to be introduced to people abroad, it became wildly popular in England, perhaps because the English gave Americans the idea for hot breakfasts with egg and ham in the first place. Herb simply returned the favor by giving that breakfast back to the Brits in a tasty new configuration. Continental Europe was another matter. In places like France and the Nordic countries, a cold breakfast, composed of pastries or sliced meats, is still the tradition. The Egg McMuffin is making inroads there, but more slowly.

A continent away, in Asia, however, the solution to breakfast may make its largest impact yet. Fittingly, Herb played a role in helping persuade the Chinese to open McDonald's restaurants there. By 1990 McDonald's had opened two restaurants in a special economic zone in China close to Hong Kong, but had yet to open any restaurants elsewhere in the country. That year, the company began talking with a prominent Chinese businessman about opening the first McDonald's in Beijing. Accustomed to a communist economic system, the businessman struggled to understand the concept of joint ownership between McDonald's and all of the restaurant operators. No matter how many people explained it to him, it still didn't make sense.

Finally, the Chinese businessman came to visit the United States. McDonald's sent him to Santa Barbara, where he sat down for lunch with Herb and David. Under a brilliant California sun, Herb broke down this strange free-market ownership structure in a way the man could understand. Then they took him to the Santa Barbara Zoo to visit the elephants, Little Mac and Sujatha, who had come all the way from Southeast Asia to make their home here.

Two years later, in April of 1992, the first Chinese McDonald's opened its doors in Beijing. Today there are more than 1,100 McDonald's restaurants across China and more than a hundred new ones opening every year. In fact, McDonald's is growing more rapidly in China than in any other country. The man who opened the first ones still keeps a photo of himself with David's daughter, Whitney, on the wall of his office.

Only in 2004 did McDonald's decide that it was finally time to introduce breakfast to its customers in China. It already had been selling breakfast to the Chinese in a small way, but that wasn't good enough for Jeff Schwartz, the CEO of McDonald's China, who—as you may recall—felt so perplexed by the very first Egg McMuffin he ever saw back in Minnesota when he was just sixteen. Decades later, Jeff knew the pan-baked muffins his Chinese restaurants were using in place of English muffins didn't cut it. Real English muffins aren't baked in a pan, but exposed directly to the fire. Until he got that part right, Jeff wasn't about to make a big deal out of the McDonald's hallmark breakfast dish. It took years to get a dedicated English muffin factory up and running outside of Shanghai, but in 2008, he finally succeeded. Now it's cranking out thousands of genuine English muffins a day. Finally the time had come to introduce the real Egg McMuffin to China in a big way.

In China Herb's creation isn't called the Egg McMuffin exactly. Instead it's called My Man Fen, which, in Mandarin, sounds a little like Egg McMuffin, but means "McDonald's perfect score," a concept familiar to every Chinese schoolkid.

In China, people are accustomed to eating their breakfasts hot. They also like their first meal of the day with eggs and ham. All this bodes well for Herb's creation. In 2007, breakfast accounted for just 3 percent of revenues for McDonald's China. In 2008, it was up to 8 percent and still climbing. In Hong Kong that number is in the low twenties, keeping pace with the U.S. market.

There are so many changes afoot in China right now that sometimes this far-off land seems to resemble the same land where Herb opened his first restaurants back in the harried 1970s. The only thing is that there are many, *many* more growling stomachs to feed in the morning—one for each of the one billion people there, the largest population of any country on the planet. In fact, in China, a vast new horizon stretches out before Herb's humble creation.

∞ ∞ ∞

Not many people know the story of Herb and the Egg McMuffin, nor do they know all the lessons both have to teach about innovation, courage, perseverance and taking care of others.

Those who do know, however, see much more than a meal every time they enjoy Herb's solution to the problem with breakfast. Out in Overland Park, Kansas, Dan Deeble smiled recently when his local McDonald's displayed a picture of an old convertible with a McMuffin license plate in its lobby. It reminded him of the EGG MC1 license plate on Mr. P's green Cadillac. Even though ten years have passed since he'd worked with Herb, Dan hasn't forgotten all he'd learned from Herb, David and Monte. Sometimes, as he plays Frisbee golf around the church grounds, the memory of Herb and his time at McDonald's gives him an idea or two for his next sermon.

And you know Herb's smiling about that.

ALL THE YOLKS OF THE MATTER

1. Heed the hunger.

2. Dreams are great—if you're sleeping. But to make them come true, you have to be awake.

3. To find your way, sometimes you have to go out of your way.

4. Sometimes it takes new shapes to contain new ideas.

5. One man's sauce is another man's cheese

6. The road to success is paved with mentors. Find yours.

7. Timing isn't everything, but without it, your hard work may amount to nothing.

8. When you've got your ducks in a row, make sure one of them is a really big duck.

9. Be conscientious about your "objectors."

10. If you're going to be the star, make sure you know your lines.

11. Fall in love with the first name if you must, but marry the one that will last forever.

12. Hold tight til it's right, and then let it go to watch it grow.

13. The restaurant business doesn't serve just food, but also people.

14. Share the eggs in your basket.

15. Your work is your ministry. Put your heart at the center of it.

16. Nothing's more valuable than your values.

17. Hatch a batch of happiness.

18. When you take care of people, they take care of you—and many others, too.

19. Be a good egg.

NOTES

CHAPTER 2
1. Maryann Tebben, "History of French Fries," *Convivium Artium: Food Representation in Literature, Film, and the Arts,* Spring, 2006, http://flan.utsa.edu/conviviummartium/Tebben.html.

2. Belgium Tourist Office, "History of French Fries," www.visitbelgium.com.

3. The American Folklife Center online, "Inventor of the Hamburger, Louis Lassen," http://lcweb2.loc.gov/diglib/legacies/CT/200002814.html.

4. State of Connecticut, "Inventor of the Hamburger, Louis Lassen," http://www.ct.gov/ctportal/cwp/view.asp?a=843&q=246434

CHAPTER 3
1. Elizabeth David. *History of English Muffins: English Bread and Yeast Cookery* (New York: Penguin, 1979), 345-346, 348-349.

2. Bays English Muffins, "History of English Muffins," www.bays.com/history/.

CHAPTER 9
1. Claudia O'Donnell (editor-in-chief, *Prepared Foods*), in discussion with the authors, October 2009.

2. Martin Friedman, "New Food Products – Product Launches that Failed," *Prepared Foods*, April 15, 1994, www.preparedfoods.com.

CHAPTER 11
1. John F. Love, *Behind the Arches* (New York: Bantam Books, 1986), 300.

CHAPTER 14
1. History of Peleliu, www.militaryhistoryonline.com.

2. Bill Sloan, *Brotherhood of Heroes: The Marines at Peleliu, 1944—The Bloodiest Battle of the Pacific War* (New York: Simon & Schuster, 2006), 310–315.

ACKNOWLEDGMENTS

There are so many people I want to thank for the roles they have played in my life and for all they have contributed to *The Good Egg*.

The first is my mother, who showed me so much love and was always my biggest cheerleader. In an era when divorce has become the norm, the way that my parents loved each other for sixty-three years was such an inspiration.

To my wonderful, spirited wife, Sue, for your unwavering support of all I do. I always know you are behind me and I am so grateful that you have always encouraged me to pursue our dreams.

To our amazing kids Whitney, Parker and Lakey—your grandfather left you a wonderful legacy of joy and living life to the fullest. He loved you all so much. To the greatest son-in-law in the world, Matt Eves, you made it easy for me to give away my daughter. Welcome to the family.

To my sisters Sally Crispin, Susan Kelly and Barbie Witmer, who are all about laughter and celebration—just like our parents. As your younger brother, I've had fun celebrating life with you. I look forward to keeping alive our parents' tradition of large and frequent family get-togethers.

To my brother-in-law Bob Kelly, who was there when Dad created the Egg McMuffin, your insights and memories have been invaluable. To Bill Crispin and Brad Witmer, Dad loved the grandkids you gave him.

To all of my amazing nieces and nephews: Beth, Heather, Jennifer, Katie, Lauren, Lindsay, Megan and Peter. You brought "Bebop" to life and were the apple of his eye.

To Ray Kroc, the original "Danny Dreamer," whose vision and passion for one simple hamburger stand launched one of the most recognizable brands around the world. My dad loved you so very much.

To Fred Turner, whose unique partnership with Ray built the Golden Arches into the exceptional company we know today. Thank you for caring so much about this project, and especially for giving the Egg McMuffin the go-ahead. And to your wife Patty, who came up with its one-of-a-kind name. This book would not have come to be without you.

To Jeff Schwartz, I'm forever grateful for your passion, great sense of humor and incredible support as a friend and colleague.

To Paul Schrage, one of my father's closest friends and compatriots, for being the marketing mastermind behind the incredible McDonald's brand worldwide, and for your love of the Egg McMuffin story and of my father.

To my father's longtime friend Al Golin, for all your help in recalling the day of the all-important cooking demonstration.

To Monte Fraker, boy, we've been through so much together. Thank you for being the closest of friends and an equal partner. It's been amazing having you as a teammate.

To Dan Deeble, for the unbelievable effort you put into this book. For your laughter, fun, creativity and for living your faith through your actions and kindness.

To my fellow owner-operators throughout the United States, with whom I've worked since I was ten years old. There are dozens of you who have influenced me, including the Paschens, the Madduxes, the Pernickys, the Lopatys, Ti Chang, Glen Cook and the list goes on and on.

To everyone at McDonald's headquarters in Oak Brook, Illinois, who provided logistical and research help, as well as their enthusiasm: Mike Bullington, Joyce Molinaro, Jennifer O'Malley and Danya Proud, among many others.

To all the great folks at the Rick Johnson Agency, including Rick and Debbie Johnson, Pam Schneider and, especially, to Jessica Trumble, for the care and thoughtfulness you invested in all your edits to the book.

To my coauthor Ann Marsh—when we first met, you grasped my dad's story right away and envisioned an inspiring way to share it with the world. Thank you for your enthusiasm. You became enamored with my Dad's story and became an intregal part of my life and family. I'm looking forward to being friends forever. My dad would have loved you and thought were a good egg.

To our editor and guiding light Richard Rosen. Before we met you, we were searching for the right direction. You gave us the right focus, format and voice to tell Dad's story. Your instincts are unerring. I am in awe of your imagination.

To Patrick Borelli, for your visual gifts, and to Judy Pray, for your professionalism, in bringing this book over the finish line.

I cannot say enough about the thousands and thousands of dedicated managers and team members who have worked with us at Santa Barbara McDonald's over the last forty years. Thank you! In particular, I want to thank CC Doctolero, Harry Fountain, Marco Gavilanes, Karrie Mata, Danny Monarres, Omar Santos, Javier Diaz and Gaby Velazquez. You are the reason that there is story to tell about the Egg McMuffin.

To Agustin DeGuevara, who is a great lover of all people, for your many years of service and for bringing great heart and soul into our organization as our unofficial chaplain.

And, of course, to the countless customers who come through the doors of our restaurants every day. You are the reason behind all we do. When I think of our customers, I think of people like Cesar Usaka, who joined us every single day for his daily Egg McMuffin and large coffee (taken with two creams and one sugar) for more than thirty years until the day he passed away.

My parents taught me the value of friendship. My dad always said if you have five close friends at the end of your life, you are a lucky person. I am so blessed to have so many great friends. In particular, I want to thank a few of them, including Lindsay Parton, one of the most encouraging people I know and as true a friend as can be; Kelly and Ray George and their beautiful kids, your family defines love and friendship; the Ryan family—we can't wait to grow old with you on a deserted tropical beach; and Jay Carty, your books have touched me and I hope I did you proud.

Lastly, I want to thank not only my father who raised me, but my heavenly father whose love and peace surpass all understanding.

ABOUT THE AUTHORS

Working alongside his father for more than thirty years, DAVID PETERSON turned his family's six McDonald's restaurants into one of the company's most admired and emulated franchises. In particular, McDonald's of Santa Barbara and Goleta is widely respected for the way it treats its team members and invests in its local community.

ANN MARSH is a columnist with the *Los Angeles Times* and a former staff writer for *Forbes* magazine. The coauthor of two other books, she is based out of Los Angeles.